Entrepreneur

Vs

Serial Entrepreneur

Angry Kawk

No part of this Book may be reproduced or transmitted in any form or by any means, electronic or mechanical, including photocopying, recording or by any information storage and retrieval system, without written permission from the author.

These rants are purely what is off the top of my head. I set an hour glass upside down, and just go. No looking back, no thinking too far ahead. I hope they can be a little informative, along with entertaining.

Ok, the hour glass is turned, and here we go.

"Serial Entrepreneur vs Real Entrepreneur. I think if we have got time, we can maybe throw in another one. And that is the "wannapreneur", which makes up most of the people who think they are actually real entrepreneurs.

Which makes it oh so funny for people like us.

What is the first thing you think of, when seeing the word serial?

I guarantee, 90% + of people, will automatically say serial killer, right? I bet it's closer to 99%.

Well, that's not far off from what a serial entrepreneur is, somewhere inside of them. Most of them are probably closer to a serial killer, than an actual entrepreneur.

These people are obsessive, selfish, myopic, train wrecks of human beings.

Don't be one of them. Even if you are a wannapreneur, and just cannot seem to not get scammed over, and over again.

Never identify yourself as a frikin serial entrepreneur.

It comes off desperate, and crack addict – ish.

Seriously, these people are spinning their wheels. And many will end up with all kinds of anxiety issues that they cannot ever reverse.

Oh yea, and let's not forget to mention, broke. They all end up broke, when it's all said and done.

The way the internet allows shiny pieces of shit, to appear to be gold, now days. It will only make it worse.

And the con artists of now, and the future, are salivating, at the chance to pop all these new virgin cherries that are just bending over, and spreading butt cheeks, waiting for them to come & stick it in.

It is equally hilarious, and sad, all at the same time.

I feel for people who get ramrodded by cons. On the other hand, I could not give 2 shits.

This is how I stay sane through it all. It is the only way to. Especially if you care, and do your best to not deceive people, in order to make your money. If you care too much, it brings you down along with them. Serial entrepreneur is a buzz term, I have seen around a lot the last half a decade especially.

I have no clue how long dumb asses have been using it? But, I see it used more & more now, with pride, in defining themselves as this go getter.

Hustler. Money making machine.

Yea, yea, go fuck yourself.

We are in a new era of "entrepreneurship". And a completely new technology driven world, that is perfect for evil con artists, to capture their victims without breaking a sweat.

It is so easy now, that it is not even a chase anymore for them. The dipshits go to them. Youtube, Instagram, and the rest, are to thank for this.

For the time being of course. Things will change, and they will have to reinvent, or regroup, and come up with new strategies to lure people in.

But right now, it is easy pickings for them. Because they can target kids (young males) more than ever.

See, waaaaay back in the old days. Like even in the early 2000's. It was still the old blue haired fogies, that took the brunt of the butt fucking.

Yea, they still are a good target for bullshit mlm, and some other types of hilarious scams.

But things have shifted over to targeting young, dumb, full of cum, little boys, who still are learning how to shave their little non dropped balls.

These are the clowns that eventually start calling themselves serial entrepreneurs, and post all these dumb fucking memes on social media.

The ones who are always cheering these desperate people on, are of course, the ones who are extracting money from them in some way.

Convincing them, that they are destined for a lifestyle of freedom, and calling their own shots. Blah, blah, blah.

Fire your boss!

Quit your job!

Escape the 9 to 5!

And the list goes on, and no right? Those of us who have been around block, after block (doesn't matter the age). And probably one time fell for these things. Know exactly what is what, right?

I am sure that most people reading this do? So it appears, that simply putting the words, serial entrepreneur, in your Instagram description, automatically means that you are some kind of multi - millionaire, successful guru of some sort? Because this is how it appears to be. Is this "hating", as they like to quickly say all over the internet these days?

Am I a "hater"?

I consider myself, more of a healer, or helper. But, whatever makes people feel all warm and fuzzy inside...

The internet is a scary thing. It can lead us to believe that fantasy, is actually reality.

Right now, as we speak.

It is somewhat the wild west, as it is not really regulated for the time being.

Scammers of all kinds, can pretty much have their pickings of brain dead morons.

This will eventually change.

But I don't think anytime soon. So plan on this going on for some time to come.

It is one of those shit has to hit the fan type of ordeals.

Some serious shit has to really hit the fan, in order to get the attention of those who control all of us, to eliminate something that we, as Lilliputians, see as powerful, or a force to be reckoned with.

"Powers that be", don't like that shit.

They are the force to be reckoned with. And if another force oversteps its authority, they wack it.

Understand, that people can dance around the meadows, all day long, skipping, and hopping around, in wannapreneur – land, posing as millionaires, and billionaires even. As long as they really aren't making any serious money. At least hoarding it.

Seriously, there are "gurus" out there, who claim to be billionaires. Bull fucking shit. Bull fucking shit, double fisted up the ass, with a twist.

Bull shit on the "laptop millionaires" as well.

Hell, bull shit on the so called six figure earners, that just love to show off their fake screenshots to lowly, uninformed, desperate, everyday 9 to 5ers, who are **JUST LIKE THEM!**

It's a fucked up world we live in. And people do what they have to do, in order to keep their own heads above the water.

If that includes using someone elses shoulders to stand on, while they drown. Then so be it.

Money, and power, are equals, when it comes to motives, that drive people to do some of the most evil natured things imaginable.

Am I venturing too far of the reservation here?

I know I am supposed to be ranting about serial entrepreneurs.

Which I am.

But I am also going a little deeper into the reason why we have dip shits so excited to call themselves serial entrepreneurs.

An entrepreneur, does not = to a person who sits on the beach, sipping margaritas with some hot skank.

Pressing a few buttons on their laptops, while these slaves from 3rd world countries do all of their dirty work for them.

In order for them to sit back, and watch the millions roll into any one of their dozen or so, bank accounts.
This is some sick dream, that we see more and more of online. In the online world.
Or "space", as these fuck wads like to say, in order to come off as intellectual.
Entrepreneurs are all around us.
They are people who own all of the stores, and shops we shop at daily.
Even the conglomerates, and entities, were at one, an entrepreneur with a dream, and balls.

Oh yea, and probably money. Because it does take money to start things, no matter what people on the internet say.

"From zero to $100,000 in 6 months!"

So this whole fantasy of online, passive income, is all one big lure, to sucker in as many people who work a day job, as possible.

Is it real?

Of course it is. I am living proof of it. I quietly make money from multiple sources of income passively, semi passively, and even more actively.

And no, these little rants do not count. I actually lose money with these.

Because I am taking an hour out of my time, to write them. When I could be spending that hour, making money.

So don't worry, for all of the people who hate to see people make a dime. (And that's a lot of damn people.

Hopefully not you?) That's about what I make with these things, if anything at all. They are purely for my own enjoyment. And hopefully, can benefit a few people in the process. At least, mildly entertain them. But I work my ass off. Both offline, and online, and everything in between , in order to make as much money as possible, ethically.

Without even having to sucker people into my funnels, and loopholes of endless how to make money bullshit.

I am nowhere near anything how to make money. I despise the "niche".

So I create real products. Real services. One's that people buy, because they are searching for these things.

Not because I lure them in with my Instagram memes, and YouTube fake screenshots of income.

I am out of that circle of death, and it feels great. I would rather have a "job", then to try and live inside of that madness. It would kill my soul. And I am a person, who prides myself on having a lot of soul.

I encourage people to avoid those traps. They are traps. And can completely ruin peoples lives, who are not quite understanding of what these things really are.

I have seen a lot of people over the years, get completely hucked.

And it sucks that there are so many people, who get away with it. Right now, more than ever.

Most of these people you see on YouTube, Facebook, Instagram, and various forums on money.

Are complete bullshiters. And some even professional bullshit artists.

Not all. But most. As in way over 95%. More like 99.9%. That's not good odds, in trying to find that .01%. So, I say don't even try.

A person who is seriously entrepreneurial, does not need anyone to charge them, in order for them to find that out.

These people are shystering people, with schemes, and dreams.

The very few people who can hack it, in any type of business, don't need those things.

Some, just aren't life experienced enough, to know this, yet. But they will. Hopefully, they do not lose too much of their hard earned money in the process.

The best thing to do, is to never trust anyone, who acts like they are put on this planet to help you make money.

Or, even help you learn how to apply some type of scheme, which, is supposed to help you make money.

You will always win, when you never play.

I know, that's the complete opposite of what these fucktards will say, right?

You can't win, if you don't play.

That's just another mind fuck, they use on the green.

Carve your own path.

And build your own business(es), whatever they may be, on legit, trustworthy, products, and/or services.

That's how you win, in the long term.

That's what the definition of an entrepreneur is.

Not some tweeked out, serial wannapreneur, living at mommy & daddies, who is so flustered in life, that they can't even function properly in the real world, before they even hit 30.

Fuck that. Fuck chasing fake dreams, and making up dumb ass goals, that are not achievable.

Anyways, my hour is up.

I hope this was moderately informative, and grossly entertaining. Vice – versa will also do.

Angry Kawk scratching out.

Don't forget to leave reviews. They are appreciated! And check out more Angry Kawk Rants on Amazon.

www.ingramcontent.com/pod-product-compliance
Lightning Source LLC
Chambersburg PA
CBHW050034230526
45470CB00003B/1271